SAWBEAR'S Orange Beach Vacation
by: Tracy Ryder Bradshaw

Written & Photographed by Tracy Ryder Bradshaw
Designed by Michael Todd Ryder
Sawbear made by Debra Reagan
Edited by Anne Horner and Corkie Staley

Sawbear Books
Sawbear's Orange Beach Vacation

Other Titles in this Series:
Sawbear Goes to a Wedding

All rights reserved. No part of this publication may be reproduced, stored in a retrieval system, or transmitted in any form or by any means - electronic, mechanical, photocopy, recording, or other except for brief quotations in written reviews, without the prior written permission of the publisher.

Sawyer Prints
301 Ravenwood Drive
Wartburg, TN 37887

www.sawyer-prints.com

ISBN: 978-1-946790-01-9

Library of Congress Control Number: **2017911597**

Manufactured in the United States of America
Text and Photographs copyright © 2017 Tracy Ryder Bradshaw
Design and Format copyright © 2017 Michael Todd Ryder

Orange Beach, here we come! I am so excited to be going on a vacation to the beach because I have never been there. I am ready with my seatbelt fastened. Who forgot to put new batteries in my keyboard? I cuddle with my favorite stuffed animal. Are we there yet? I read a book about me going to a wedding. I like that book. When am I going to see the beach? An oatmeal cream pie sure is a tasty treat. How much longer? Coloring hearts, working puzzles, and sneaking in a good nappy nap are some of my favorite things to do.

Finally there is a sign for the beach, and right away I see the Orange Beach water tower! There is the Gulf of Mexico! The trees are different than the ones at home. They are called palm trees, and I see love in them.

We are here! Finally we are at Orange Beach. I have waited all my life to see this place. First we walk through the condo and go out on the balcony. A balcony is like a porch that is high in the air. I see the most beautiful thing I have ever seen. It is the beach! Wow, there is a pool right below us too!

I want to get close to those waves, but first I look at all the pictures in the Beach Guide. There are a lot of safety rules for the beach, and one that is very important is the "SUNSCREEN" rule. Mom puts two layers of sunscreen on me. I put on my goggles, and we pack for fun at the beach!

Ouch! The sand is hot, so we walk quickly toward the water. We get close and stop. Mom draws a heart in the sand and writes my name in it. She tells me that I am in her heart. Then we plop down in the sand and build tall sandcastles. The sand is cooler where I am digging.

Oh, I love the ocean! It looks like it goes on forever because I cannot see where it ends. The sand is squishy under my feet and my bottom. Now I am ready to learn how to go "shell diving"!

I am a quick learner, and I find a lot of pretty shells. There are many different colors, shapes, sizes, and textures. Some are very smooth; some are bumpy and have spots or lines. Mom's favorites are the big pieces of sand-dollars that are shaped like hearts. She puts one on my chest because I have a big heart and she loves me.

After putting all my shells in a bucket, I stretch out on my favorite blanket to dry. The sunscreen will help keep me from getting a sunburn. The sun feels hotter at the beach than it does at home. I am glad that I read that Beach Guide.

Whew, now I need some shade. It is much cooler under the beach umbrella, and I feel the ocean breeze. I see the waves jump up, run toward me, fall down with a great crashing noise, and crawl up the sand. Then swoosh! They get sucked back out into the ocean. The air smells like salt and sand, and I like all these new things.

Surprise! We are going kayaking, and I have never been kayaking! An important rule for kayakers is to wear lifejackets! Mom puts my lifejacket on me, puts me in the kayak, and away we go! The waves make this a bouncy ride, and I am a little scared that I might pop right out of the kayak. That is why wearing a lifejacket is such an important rule. As we go a little farther out in the ocean, we get past the rough waves. The ride is smoother, and it is fun being in a kayak on the ocean!

We are hungry and thirsty after that big adventure, so we go back to the condo for lunch. We have bagels with cream cheese, some fruit, and a cold drink. I eat a lot of blueberries and some mango. Mango is a new taste for me, and it is yummy. Then we relax on the balcony for awhile.

After a good rest, we go to the pool. I try every chair to find the one I like the best. They are all great, but I love the white one! It is fun to put the back of it up, down, or in between.

There is a number six painted on the concrete. Hmmm, I wonder why that is here as I reach to touch the water. It feels great, and I stretch to make a splash. All at once I am under the water! Mom saves me with a net and explains that the six means the water is six feet deep here. That is way over my head! She says that I am not allowed in the pool without a floatation device. Now I am a little nervous about that big pool, and I think Mom is too.

After thinking in my favorite chair, I get back in the pool. I learn how to hold onto floats. I can even pull myself up out of the water. I tell Mom, "You can put away the net now!" I climb up the ladder and suddenly realize I love this pool!

I get inside a tire float and practice on a cool board. I want to know how to use these before I take them in the pool.

We leave the pool to head back to our condo, and I put on Mom's hat to shade my face. I push the button for the elevator. I am so tired that I flop down in the corner as we zoom up to the third floor. Back inside the condo, I climb up on a bright bed to rest for a minute, and I accidentally fall asleep.

I wake from another nappy nap, and I check out my tan. I love looking in the mirror, because there is only one me in the world. That makes me special. I am Sawbear!

Mom says that it is time for a bath. I'm getting in water again, but this time it is to get clean and ready for some fun running around this beach town.

I am clean and ready to go to The Wharf. It is a fun place with shopping, music, and restaurants. There is also a movie theater. I can't wait to see all of these things!

As we are leaving, I can't resist climbing this tree, because I love to climb! This kind of tree feels like a ladder with steps, and I climb high.

FERRIS WHEEL

Surprise! The Wharf has a Ferris Wheel, and I love those things! We run straight to it. After waiting for this giant wheel to quit going around and around, I climb the metal steps and get inside my very own gondola! The operator gives me the best ride of my life!

Look! I'm a fisherman, and I catch the biggest fish I've ever seen. Now I'm a lobster with claws!

I want to catch more fish, so I go fishing again. I return as a muscle man from reeling in all those huge fish!

There are many places to sit and relax. I like this white chair, but sitting on the wooden pelican is more fun!

As the sun fades and the moon peaks out, I notice that I can't stop looking back at that Ferris Wheel. It is beautiful with all the lights. There is music and a light show. Wow, the palm trees keep changing colors.

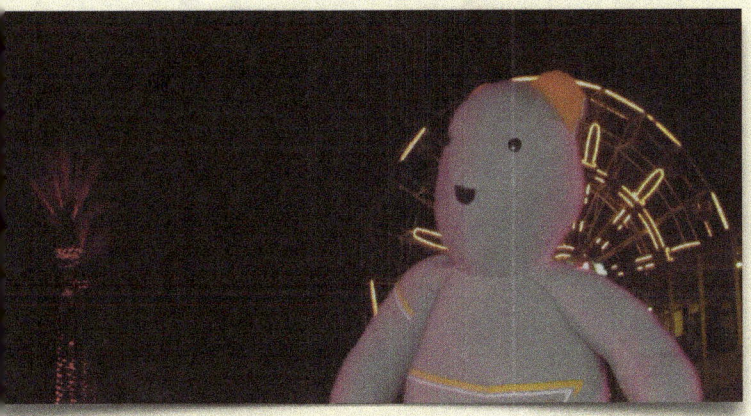

Well, this Ferris Wheel rider, fisherman, lobster, and muscle man is worn out so we drive back to the condo. I stretch out on the seashell couch, and Mom says that it is bedtime. I get in a drawer, but she takes me out. She puts me on the soft bed, cuddles with me, and laughs as she makes loud kisses all over my face. It is a happy goodnight time.

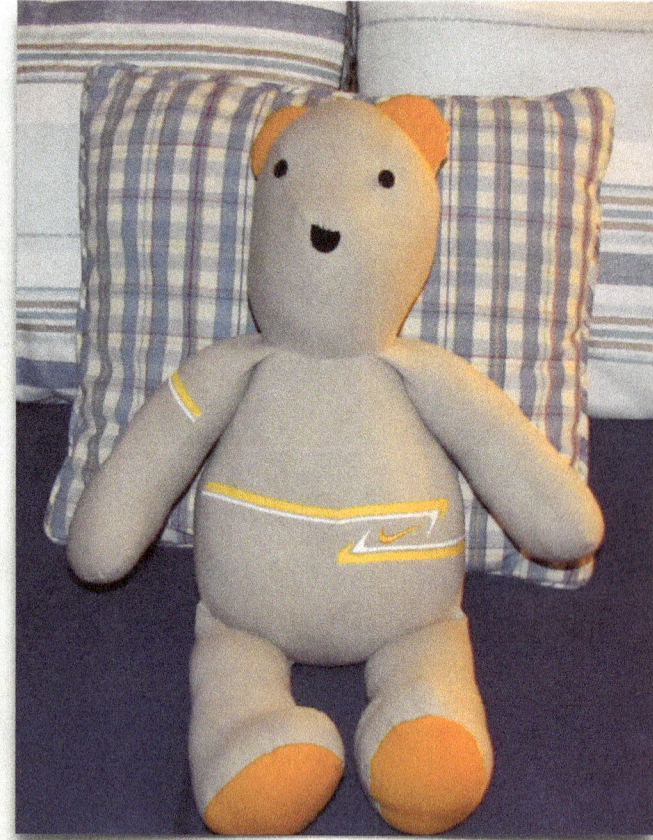

Night passed like a flash of lightning, and this morning we are grocery shopping. I help by holding the food so it won't fall out of the cart. I also give lots of suggestions about what to buy.

We finish at the store and drive back to the condo. While Mom puts away the groceries, I sit in a bowl and watch her. Then I begin climbing on things. Mom tells me that I should save my energy for the beach so I watch cartoons on TV.

When the groceries are stored, we wash the sand off all the shells. Then we pack them in plastic bags, so we can enjoy looking at our collection without scattering them all over the condo.

While waiting to go to the beach, I climb on the bunk beds and pretend I'm on a big ship looking down at the ocean. I sit in the captain's chair.

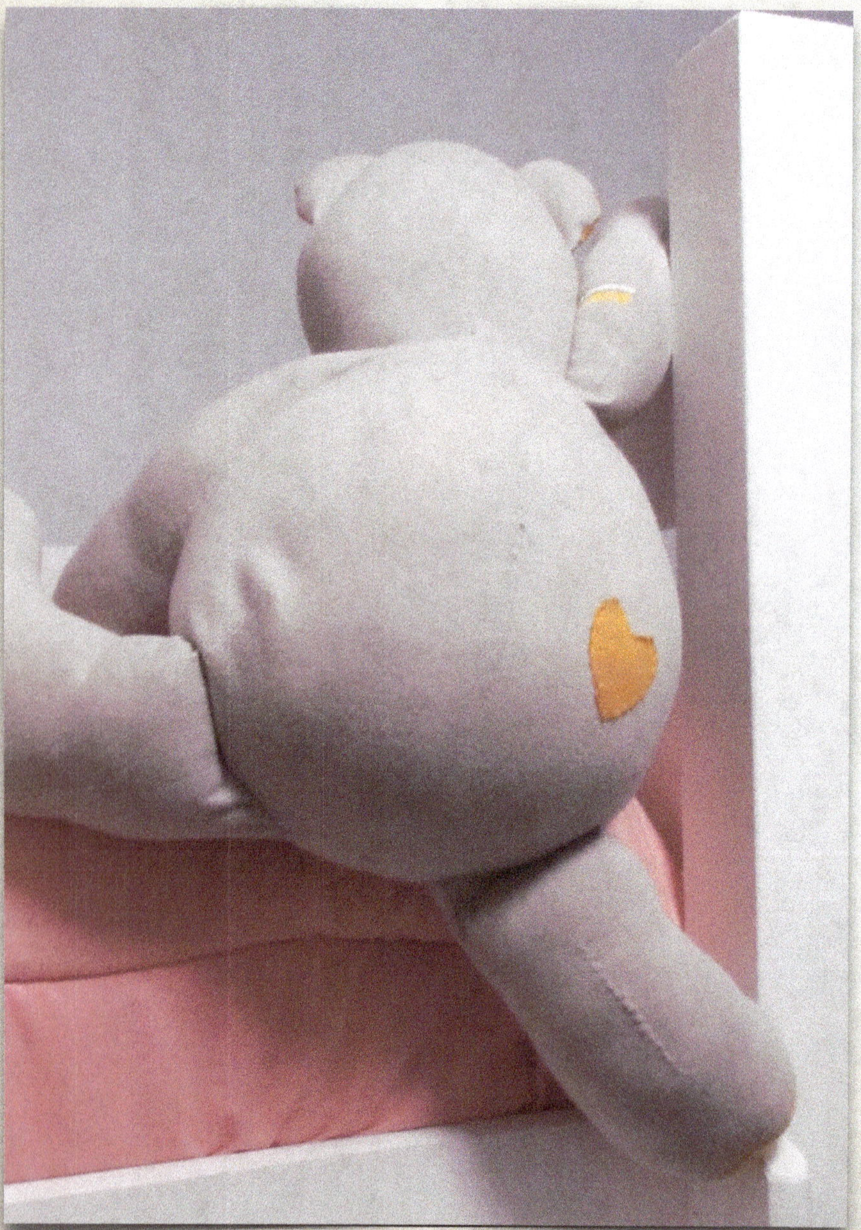

Finally I get to go back to the beach! I run ahead on the wooden path and climb up the side. It is a beautiful beach day! Close to the water, I spend hours building a great sandcastle village with a moat. I add pretty shells on a secret walkway. Then I take a break from all that work.

As the sun begins to disappear, we begin our walk back to the condo. The tall steps to the wooden path are difficult to climb at the end of a busy day at the beach.

Out on the balcony of the condo, I see the moon! It isn't even dark yet. After a bath and dinner, I go back out on the balcony. That big moon is still there. I think I love the moon.

I am squeaky clean and very tired. It is our last bedtime here, because we are leaving in the morning. I don't even make it all the way in the bed before falling asleep.

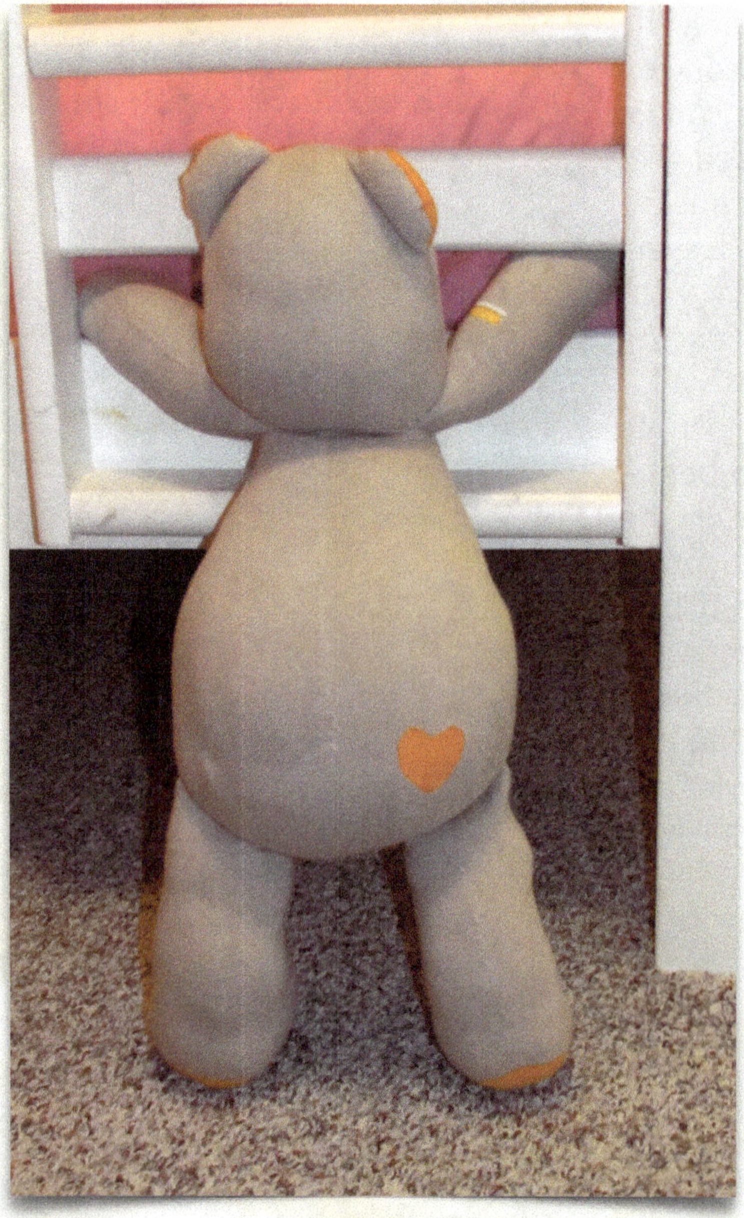

I don't want to go home today! I am blocking the door so we cannot leave. I love Orange Beach, and I want to stay. Mom promises to bring me back for another fun vacation. I get in the car for the long ride home. She hugs me and tells me her heart is happy that I had such fun. Just knowing that makes my heart happy too.

Orange Beach is my favorite vacation place, but there is nothing as comfortable as my own bed. Ahhh, I hope I dream about the beach!

www.ingramcontent.com/pod-product-compliance
Lightning Source LLC
Chambersburg PA
CBHW060504240426
43661CB00007B/906